Magical Fly Fishing for the Majestic Steelhead

by

Clay Sharp

© 2005 Clay Sharp. All Rights Reserved.

No part of this book may be reproduced, stored in a retrieval system, or transmitted by any means without the written permission of the author.

First published by AuthorHouse 03/25/05

ISBN: 1-4208-4119-X (sc)

Printed in the United States of America
Bloomington, Indiana

This book is printed on acid-free paper.

authorHOUSE

1663 LIBERTY DRIVE
BLOOMINGTON, INDIANA 47403
(800) 839-8640
www.authorhouse.com

Acknowledgements

I would like to personally thank my family and special friends who believed in me, for not giving up on me, and who inspired me to complete this project. You know who you are.

Dedication

This book is dedicated to my three incredible kids and to those who have served to ensure their freedom.

Table of Contents

Foreword vii

Introduction xi

Steelhead, The Ultimate Freshwater Game Fish In The Ultimate Country 1

Beginners Luck 7

Fly Patterns That Can! 9

Finding Those Fish, Time To Explore 26

Unlocking The Hiding Places 31

Adaptation, Another Key To Success 37

Get Ready To Rumble 43

A Wonderful Fall Day – Dreams Can Come True 47

It's The Technique, Not The Equipment 56

What Good Is Treasure If You Can't Share It 60

Foreword

When I first met Clay I figured he was like any other Steelhead fly fisherman. I was quickly convinced he wasn't after browsing a few pictures; so I bought a fly rod the very next day.

The first day I went out with Clay on the river was the first time I ever landed a Steelie on a fly. It was called the Sharp Steelie, very modern pattern. I witnessed Clay and his smooth technique land at least 15 Steelhead before I had even landed my first. I figured Clay had the best stretch on the river. Well this wasn't the case, he was yet again fighting a nice Steelie down river so I quickly moved up stream to his hole - thinking quick strike, I'll be fighting one too. He landed his chromer and immediately had another one on where I once was.

It didn't really matter where Clay fished, he scouted the water looking for rifts and holes - presented his fly, and the fight was on!

There is a reason he is nicknamed "The Machine" - I am very thankful he has shared his flies and techniques with me so that I have now had success fly fishing for Steelies, way to go!

Toby Tyler

Hello fellow Fishermen and Ladies,

My name is Steve. I have lived in the Northwest since I was born. Growing up on Whidbey Island, I have known a life time of fishing. My Dad got us started fishing early on in the lakes, rivers and the salt. I recently had the opportunity to fish with Clay Sharp in one of the feeder rivers to the Columbia. Being a confident and competitive fisherman, I'd looked forward to fishing with Clay for some time as I had seen the photos and heard the stories. The first time we fished together, we drove to one of Clay's "recommended" places and climbed down a very long and steep embankment. We looked around to check out the competition and chose our spot. I had my trusty casting Steelhead pole set with all kinds of gear. As the morning went on, I realized all my gear and ideas were quickly falling behind Clay's fly fishing technique and one small fly. It was very frustrating! As a matter of fact, I wasn't the only fishermen there getting tired of hearing "Fish On". Ok, all in all it was a good day of fishing for every one but most certainly Clay caught and released many more than I (or anyone else) caught. I took his advise to pick up a new fly rod and borrowed a few of his newly designed Sharp Steelie flies. It didn't take long to find out Clay's technique and flies were very effective with the 8 to 30 LBS Steelhead. It was one of the best river fishing weeks I had ever known only to be out done by the following years run fishing with Clay.

Sincerely,

Steve Davis

Clay:

Thanks for the tips and info. Yes, the Sharp (Steelie) has been productive for me, it's been my go-to since I started tying it.

As for stories....I got off work early one day and decided to hit the Green. All I had was my spin gear and some rags with me. There was another guy (Bobby something) using everything from Wullies to Green Butts and not getting so much as a look. I had about 20 Sharps in my vest and as we were talking I offered him a couple.

He tied on a Chartuese colored Sharp (I tie every color in the rainbow just to be safe) and on his first toss lost it in a blackberry bush. Second time around, same color, he managed to get it across and slightly upstream. I was joking with him about the creator "guaranteeing" chrome if they were anywhere in the system. He started to say something about hearing that before and WHAM! Steel on. He was so unprepared that it almost took all his backing before he started applying the brakes. It was a great fight and he finally landed a nice sized chrome.

Bobby stood there for a few seconds smiling like a maniac. He said he guessed everyone gets lucky once in a while, it's not the gear it's how close you get to the fish. Anyway, he's stripping line out getting ready for another cast (the Sharp's about 15 feet down stream from him) and, sure enough, another strike. This one takes off before he's even made his cast. Bobby grabs the line and the leader snaps. So now, there he stands with this sour look on his face and says, "Now I'll bet you'll want to sell me the rest of them, right?" I laughed and handed him my wallet.

We fished side by side for another two hours. Bobby hooked into six more Steelhead and kept two. I went 0-for-ever but had a blast watching him cast, mend, strike. When we got back to my car I showed him how to tie them. As "payment" he promised he'd make a few to hand out when he's on a stream and no-one's hooking up.

Anyway, thanks again for the tips and sharing the Sharp (Steelie) with us!

Kevin Durgin.

Introduction

You have just arrived on a pristine wild river in the great Northwest. The sun is just starting to warm up the air as you notice the incredible surroundings. You take a sip of coffee while contemplating the day ahead. As you're putting on your waders you notice a mule deer climbing a steep grade on the opposite bank of the river, the day is already great. While preparing the rest of the gear you are keeping an eye on the glacial fed river for any signs of activity and notice the tail of a fish breaks the surface of the water - the fish are in.

You're now wading out for the first cast of the day - just as you are casting you notice a dark object out of the corner of your eye. As the object approaches you can now tell it is some type of large bird. The bird is now flying low within 25 feet of your position and you notice a golden crown on top of its head. The bird has an enormous wingspan - you then recognize it, it is a Golden Eagle.

While your lost in the moment, all of a sudden your fly line tightens and a chrome bright fish erupts from the water. The fish quickly takes your fly line down to the backing and the battle is on - what a moment!

The fish fights brilliantly; making several amazing leaps as it try's to escape. The battle lasts for what seems like an eternity. After several minutes of pure excitement the fish finally succumbs. You admire the beautiful native for a minute, and then carefully set her free.

After the exhilarating action, you take a break to get another sip of coffee. As you're sipping the coffee you again take in the landscape that surrounds you - what a day. Now that's what fly-fishing for Steelhead is all about!

A ghostly silhouette heads upriver

Steelhead, The Ultimate Freshwater Game Fish In The Ultimate Country

    When it comes to fly fishing, there is nothing that can compare to hooking a chrome bright Steelhead in a wild scenic river. It is truly a spiritual awakening that everyone fly fishing should experience. Not only is this fish extremely powerful it is also one of nature's great works of art. Pound for pound, no other fish in fresh water can put up a battle like the Steelhead, and that is amplified ten fold when on a fly.
    I have had the opportunity to fly fish for just about every type of freshwater fish in North America and in my opinion the Steelhead is the ultimate. After a few successful days fly fishing for this fish, it's actually hard for me to go after anything else. Nothing in fly fishing compares to the thrill of this fish exploding on a fly at the surface of the water with a breath taking run to follow.
    Steelhead are turbo-charged Rainbow Trout with a taste for migration. These fish will spend one or two years as fry in their freshwater home before heading for the ocean. The fish also now reside in the Great Lakes region of the United States. Most fish will spend a few years at sea were they put on some size before returning to their home rivers to spawn. Some fish known as B-runs will spend four and vary rarely five years at sea. These fish can easily exceed 15 to 20 pounds in weight with a few fish actually reaching 30 pounds. Not all Steelhead die after spawning, unlike their Pacific Salmon cousins. Some fish may even actually return to the sea and back to spawn again.

  Luckily for anglers, the Steelhead is found in some of the most spectacular country and rivers.
  The fish inhabit many of the streams and rivers along the Pacific Northwest, British Columbia, Alaska, the Great Lakes, Russia, and even parts of South America. This champion of anadromous fish will even travel as far inland as Idaho in the Pacific Northwest.

  Being able just to drive through the Columbia River Gorge while searching for rivers with fish is a treat in itself. You really can't go wrong.
  There are two significant runs of Steelhead, summer and winter runs. In some areas you can actually find fish year round. As the run starts to slow in one river it will pick up in another as the fish migrate. A great example is the Columbia and Snake River systems in the Pacific Northwest. Just as summer run fish are making it to Idaho, Northeast Oregon, and Southeast Washington some winter runs are starting to enter the Columbia River and tributaries near it's mouth.
  Weather and water temperature can actually affect Steelhead runs. Steelhead prefer cooler water and sometimes it takes a good rain to get fish moving into home rivers. A couple clear days after some serious rain can be magical as the rivers start to drop.

    It's really hard to imagine anything better than being on a river with incredible scenery, Eagles and Osprey soaring above. Getting to watch River Otters playing along the river. Sometimes Deer and Elk coming down for a drink. Even an occasional Black Bear showing itself. All the while searching for the ultimate freshwater fish, the Steelhead.

Leaping Fury

Beginners Luck

While I was in High School my Spanish Teacher got me into the fine art of fly fishing and fly tying in New Mexico. I had the opportunity to fish several rivers including the San Juan, upper Rio Grande, and some of the other small rivers. At the time anything over 3 pounds was a great fish anywhere in the State. Find it amazing that the largest trout I ever landed in New Mexico was a 6.5 pound rainbow of all places the spillway below Lake Cochiti. Sometimes it pays to get out and explore, experiment, and be creative.

In the fall of 1980 I joined the U.S. Coast Guard and in 1984 ended up in Seattle, Washington. I was really excited about making it to the great Northwest because I had heard all kinds of stories about the outdoors including the premier game fish, a sea run Rainbow Trout.

I didn't really get back into fly fishing until a couple years after moving to Seattle until my girlfriend at the time, who is now my wife; talked me into getting back into it. She thinks she made a big mistake - but I just happen to be very thankful.

In the early summer of 1986 I started to do some research to figure out how to fly fish for Steelhead. I had heard all kinds of stories about fisherman who had been trying to land Steelhead for years without any success. This made me a little skeptical about going after these fish because I was so used to catching a lot of smaller trout; basically getting a lot of action. Wasn't sure if I would be able to handle fishing all day without any action - oh well, had to at least give it a try.

I went to several different shops trying to figure out what was needed to go after Steelhead and was rather surprised at some of the flies used to catch them - remember I was a fly fishermen from New Mexico who used all natural insect type patterns - some of the flies just plain scared me. They were all of these large bright patterns that I thought would scare a trout to death. Well after talking to several people at several shops I found out that a couple of the more effective patterns for the summer fish was the Green Butted Skunk and the Skykomish Sunrise.

Well one of my favorites as a back up fly while fishing in New Mexico was a small wooly worm. Figured I would tie up some size 8 wooly worms with a little bit of green on the butt just to see what would happen. Of course I also tied up some Green Butted Skunk's and Skykomish Sunrise's just to have a few different patterns to head out to the river.

My first fly fishing outfit consisted of a 9 foot 8 weight graphite fly rod, simple fly reel with a prawl drag, and a Cortland 15 ft sink tip fly line. Nothing real fancy, the fly reel basically had no drag to fight big fish - well it did hold plenty of backing at least. Also had various tippet materials from 0x through 3x along with some tapered leaders.

All right, now had some flies and an outfit, now it was time to head out. Decided to go to the North Fork of the Stillaquamish river, which had a fly fishing only section. I was so excited to get out that I actually couldn't sleep the night before and ended up over sleeping in the morning. Several shops told me that it was really important to get on the rivers at the crack of dawn. Well bummer, was on the road at 9 am heading for the river.

It's now around 10:30 am and I finally got on the river. It was a medium sized river with some pools here and there. While I was starting to explore, ran into another fly fishermen and asked him how he was doing and if there was any fish in the river. He told me he

hadn't landed anything this morning and he thought there was a couple fish holding in a pool just a couple yards upriver - he pointed the pool out to me and he told me to go give it try. He had tried several different flies and couldn't get anything to bite.

I tied on my wooly creation and headed to the pool. The water was swirling slowly in this pool that was about I'm guessing 50ft around. Not sure how deep it was because I couldn't make out the bottom - didn't have polarized glasses. Made my first cast upriver and the swirling current sucked my fly and fly line down towards the bottom. Within about 5 seconds after the fly hit the water - a 10-12 pound chrome bright fish exploded out of the water with my fly line attached.

Think I went into a momentary state of shock! The fish proceeded to scream upriver and had me down to my backing within seconds. Quickly figured out that I was going to have to chase the thing because my line was going to run out. And chase I did, that fish must have run me at least a couple hundred yards upriver with me frantically trying to keep up. The fish then pulled a fast one (before I could catch up) it turned and ran down river at about the same pace and jumping about every 5 seconds. The fish went back through the pool where it was hooked and preceded another hundred yards or so below the pool. Again I managed to catch back up and amazingly the fish was still on. As soon as I got parallel with the fish it took off again upriver - guess this one decided to make sure I got my run in for the day – holy cow! The chrome speedster eventually went back into the pool where it was initially hooked. After about 20-25 minutes, which seemed like eternity, I landed my first Steelhead. You know, by all rights that fish had actually won the battle. By some odd stroke of luck I think it landed itself! I admired the Steelhead for a few minutes then set her free. Was now hooked forever!

That same day I had managed to land three more fish and lost one. This had to be my most memorable day of fly fishing in my life even though it was far from the most successful. To this day my little wooly worm creation is by far my most sentimental fly and has always gotten me into summer runs.

On this day I had learned several very important keys: don't be afraid to be creative, the time of day doesn't really matter when fly fishing for Steelhead, if there is fish in the river, you can get them with a fly, and keep it simple.

Fly Patterns That Can!

One great thing about enjoying tying your own flies is getting to be creative. Every once in a while you can get lucky and come up with something that can be amazingly effective. It has always been in the back of my mind that a Steelhead is a Rainbow Trout. When you fish for Rainbow's, matching the hatch can really make the difference in success. The same is true for Steelhead!

Moving on from "Beginners Luck", the challenge of learning and creating flies to entice the fish of legend continues.

While living in the Seattle area and fishing the Puget Sound Rivers I tried a few different fly patterns and narrowed it down to some "go to" flies. Had already figured out that wooly worms and also wooly buggers worked fine for the summer run fish. During the winter runs figured out that the egg type patterns such as the Polar Shrimp would work. I was having fun and catching plenty of fish so did not really do all that much experimenting. That quickly changed when we moved to Gearhart, Oregon.

This is the first fly pattern that I came up with for Steelhead. It is my sentimental favorite because of that first magical day. Simply put, it is a Green Butted Wooly Worm that has been effective for Summer Runs throughout the years:

Hook: Mustad 79580 Streamer Hook size 6 and 8
Abdomen: Chartreuse number 2 Chenille
Body: Black number 2 Chenille
Hackle: Natural Grizzly Saddle
Thread: Black Nylon

Tying the fly:

Step One: Wind a couple wraps of thread near the bend of the hook.

Step Two: Attach the small end of natural grizzly saddle hackle near the bend of the hook and secure.

Step Three: Attach chartreuse (green) chenille near the bend of the hook and wrap tightly 2 turns. Secure with thread.

Step Four: Attach black chenille and wrap tightly up to slightly behind the eye of the hook. Secure with thread.

Step Five: Wind thread back towards the middle of the body. Wind saddle hackle towards the eye of the hook. Make one wrap with thread to secure hackle at mid body. Wind thread back towards the eye of the hook. Continue wrapping saddle hackle towards the eye of the hook. Secure with thread.

Step Six: Make enough wraps with thread at the eye to secure saddle hackle and the body.

Step Seven: Whip finish and secure with a touch of head cement.

      Green Butted Wooly Worm   Passion Fly

Next stop Gearhart, Oregon and some amazing discoveries!

    After moving to Gearhart, I decided to try and do some fishing for Sea Run Cutthroat Trout. The coastal rivers are known for this scrappy trout so it was time to come up with some fly patterns to go after them with. One of these fly patterns I now call the "Passion Fly" It's fun time!
    It's late fall in Gearhart and the weather was perfect. Calm wind, some rare sunshine, and air temps in the high 50's. I had tied up a dozen or so flies the night before so it was time to go try them out. Grabbed a 5 weight and 7 weight fly rods, loaded up the canoe, and off to the river to try and find some fish.
    It was a short drive to the river and I was just happy to get out, especially with the nice break in the weather. After looking around, I located a good area to off load the canoe, grabbed the fly rods, a small anchor, and life jacket. Just before hitting the water, set up my 5 weight so it would be ready for action. I took a deep breath of the fresh cool autumn air, took in my surroundings, and off I went.
    I just had this gut feeling it was going to be a special day.
    The river was like glass and the canoe sliced through it with little effort. I paddled towards an area where a large creek entered the main river. This area was also close to the ocean and was affected by the tides. You could hear the roar of the ocean in background while transiting pristine calm waters; oh it was wonderful!
    As I reached my destination, was going to get close to some cut banks to try and find some Cutthroats. Just as I started towards the bank something told me to look over the side into the gin clear water.

Holy crap! My hands quickly started to tremble with excitement and anxiety. I had paddled smack dab on top of what must have been easily 150 to 200 fish. They appeared to be larger than the Cutthroats and I could not clearly make out exactly what type of fish they where. I took a deep breath to try and calm myself, I was a nervous wreck!

Somehow, managed to lower the little make shift anchor without spooking the fish below. As calmly as possible, set up my 7 weight while trying not to make a lot of noise. Uh oh, all I had for flies where the ones I tied up for the Sea Run Cutthroat Trout – oh I sure hope they are going to work!

I tied on a Passion fly and nervously cast my fly line to the quarry below. The fly gently hit the water and I found myself counting in my head; one one thousand, two one thousand, three one thousand when a fish inhaled the fly! The calm that was, was no more.

The fish quickly went airborne and headed for the ocean all the while throwing me into momentary shock – It's a Steelhead! They are all Steelhead below me. Wow! Okay, quickly back to reality. Have a fish to fight.

I had to pull up the anchor while trying to hang onto a fresh, very angry Steelie on the other end. The fish gave me a wonderful battle and almost made it into the surf around the corner before finally succumbing. Oh it's going to be an incredible day.

After the energetic battle, I paddled back to the same area and the fish where still there. Again, I calmly anchored, set up, and made another cast. One one thousand, two one thousand, fish number two was in the air! Up came the anchor again and the fight was on. After another wonderful battle, the fish eventually gave in.

The same scenario continued for many furious hours of fly fishing. The fish never spooked and stayed in the area. I was having so much fun that I had completely lost track of time. All of a sudden it was dark and getting cold really quick. The day of dreams had to come to an end.

As I paddled back towards the truck became lost in deep euphoria. Once again the hands began to tremble over the thought of what had just happened. In one single day I may have just got into more fish that I thought ever possible – on a simple little fly that was made for a Sea Run Cutthroat. It was just the beginning.

The Passion Fly:

Hook: TMC or Targus 2457 size 8 and 6
Tail: Pink or light pink Saddle Hackle
Body: Multi-pink colored Wool Yarn
Collar: Natural Grizzly Saddle Hackle
Thread: Pink or red Nylon

Tying the fly:

Step One: Wind a couple wraps of thread near the bend of the hook.

Step Two: Attach 5 to 6 fibers of saddle hackle near the bend of the hook. Secure with a couple wraps of thread. Make on wrap of thread under the saddle hackle.

Step Three: Attach wool yarn near the bend of the hook and secure with a couple wraps of thread. Wind thread towards the hook eye.

Step Four: Wrap the wool yarn tightly towards the hook eye. Secure with three wraps of thread. (make sure to leave enough room for collar and head).

Step Five: Attach grizzly hackle near the hook eye with thread. Make 2 or 3 wraps of the saddle hackle and secure with thread.

Step Six: Palmer hackle slightly back in the direction of the hook bend. Secure with thread.

Step Seven: Wrap enough thread to build up head.

Step Eight: Whip finish (or 5 to 6 half hitches). Add a touch of head cement. Trim any excess material if necessary.

After such an amazing day, I had to do some research to find out why the heck such a simple fly worked so well. This is what I found out:

Throughout the Steelhead's life cycle they feed on a variety of aquatic organism's. As a smolt, the fish will feed primarily on aquatic invertebrates and also fish eggs. When the fish migrate to the ocean they will primarily feed on various forms of Zooplankton, Pelagic Worms (Larvae), and also small Squid. The exception is the Great Lakes where the fish will feed on Mysis Shrimp along with Alewives. Upon returning to their home rivers, the fish will still at times actually feed. Matching the hatch can really be effective!

Armed with this new knowledge, just had to come up with another new pattern. Made a trip to a fly shop and while looking around spotted some pinkish colored material called frost bite sparkle braid. What the heck, I had to try it out for the fly body. Buzzed up another fly pattern.

The Reflector:

Hook: TMC or Targus 2457 size 8 and 6
Tail: Pink or light pink Saddle Hackle (Can substitute 4 Strand Floss)
Body: Sparkle Braid, light pink
Collar: Natural Grizzly Saddle Hackle
Thread: Red or pink Nylon

Tying the fly:

Step One: Wind a couple wraps of thread near the bend of the hook.

Step Two: Attach saddle hackle (or floss) near the bend of the hook. Secure with 2 or 3 wraps of thread.

Step Three: Attach sparkle braid near the bend of the hook. Secure with 2 or 3 wraps of thread.

Step Four: Wind thread towards the hook eye.

Step Five: Wrap the sparkle braid (tightly) towards the hook eye. Be careful to leave enough room for head and collar.

Step Six: Wrap sparkle braid back towards middle of the body.

Step Seven: Wrap sparkle braid (tightly) back towards the hook eye to give the body a tapered appearance. Secure with 2 or 3 wraps of thread.

Step Eight: Attach saddle hackle near the hook eye and secure with thread.

Step Nine: Make 2 or 3 wraps with the saddle hackle. Secure with 2 or 3 wraps of thread.

Step Ten: Palmer hackle slightly towards the bend of the hook. Secure with thread. Make enough wraps with the thread to build up the head.

Step Eleven: Whip finish and add a touch of head cement. Cut any excess material.

Brown Steelie Nymph   Reflector

Okay, with all the newly learned knowledge it was time to do some serious experimenting. My time spent living along the Oregon Coast in Gearhart proved to be extremely valuable.

Along with the Passion fly, the Reflector, I decided to compare some old favorite's. I would bring along patterns such as; the Hairs Ear Nymph, Polar Shrimp, Wooly Worms, Wooly Buggers, Pheasant Tail Nymph, Elk Hair Caddis, and some dry Stone Fly imitations. Along with these patterns, I would bring along some traditional Steelhead flies and Atlantic Salmon flies. The results ended up backing up that matching the hatch is extremely important. The Passion Fly and Reflector produced the majority of takes.

A beautiful Steelhead that found a Brown Steelie Nymph irresistible

This very large Native about to be released was taken on a Green Sharp Steelie

for both summer and winter run fish. The nymph patterns, Wooly Worm's, and Wooly Bugger's did well for Summer runs. The egg patterns worked on winter runs. The dry fly patterns did produce some fish that where holding in shallow tail outs, and riffle type water. Fish on the traditional Steelhead patterns and Atlantic Salmon patterns where few and far between. Quickly came to the conclusion that Steelhead will actually feed and that fly patterns that can imitate a food source produce more takes.

Alright, next stop Portland Oregon and another fly that really does the job.

I had just got one of those last minute opportunities to go check out one of the great Eastern Oregon lakes. I did not have a lot of time so quickly buzzed up some simple nymphs on a streamer hook for the lake. The pattern worked fine on the lake and produced some nice Rainbow's. There was a few left over from the trip so I figured might as well give them a go for some Steelhead.

Well, the opportunity came to give this simple nymph pattern a go on the famous Deschutes river. It was another wonderful early fall day (what day is not wonderful on the Deschutes) and I had already brought some fish to hand. I had lost a few more flies than normal and basically ran out of a couple go to patterns. Time to try out the nymph.

The first area that I tried it ended up producing a couple really pretty small red sides. Have to tell you, some of those Rainbow's are absolutely stunning! After working the run pretty hard without producing any Steelhead I moved on to another area.

Eureka! First cast in the very next tail out a Steelhead did its thing.

A fresh chrome bright fish on the Deschutes can leave you speechless. Let's just say I had to break out the running wading boots. There is a reason I like to wear shorts vice waders when it's not to cold! Just can't run fast enough with the waders. By the end of the day, several fish had come to hand. Just a little more evidence that simple and natural are the way to go when it comes to fly patterns for Steelhead.

Brown Steelie Nymph:

Hook: Mustad 79580 Streamer Hook size 8 and 6
Tail: Dark Elk
Body: Natural Rabbit Dubbing
Legs: Dark Elk
Thread: Black Nylon

Tying the fly:

Step One: Wind a couple wraps of thread near the bend of the hook.

Step Two: Attach elk hair (half the length of hook shank) near the bend of the hook. Secure with thread.

Step Three: Spin rabbit dubbing onto thread – wrap towards hook eye.

Step Four: Wrap back towards middle of body (with rabbit dubbing).

Step Five: Wrap back towards hook eye with rabbit dubbing to give the body a tapered appearance.

Step Six: Attach elk hair underneath eye of hook for legs. Secure with thread so the legs are positioned towards the hook point.

Step Seven: Make several wraps with the thread at the hook eye to build up the head. Whip finish and add a touch of head cement.

As time moved on and the family was getting more and more active; I was starting to loose some precious fly tying time. Personally, would much rather spend time actually fishing than tying.

On another trip to a fly shop, I was looking around and noticed some four strand floss which got me thinking. I had used floss in the past on some other type fly patterns, and wondered how it would hold up completely on it's own. The material that I was looking at had a wonderful translucent appearance and was not too brightly colored. Hmmm, this stuff might just have potential. I picked up a couple spools; light pink and olive green, and headed home.

That same evening I buzzed up some flies with grizzly hackle for the collar. After tying the first fly, I took one look at it and just knew it would work! The fly had the potential of imitating a variety of food sources and was very quick to tie. As a bonus, it was also a fly pattern that I did not have to worry about loosing on snags etc. I would put it to the test at the first opportunity.

Well, the first opportunity came and the fly brought in 6 Steelhead to hand in a period of 4 hours. On the second opportunity using the fly, 11 Steelhead to hand. On the third opportunity – lost count after 10. Okay, this one is going to give the Passion fly some serious competition, and it did!

By the end of the fall, the fly had gotten me into so many fish that I had to take a break during the winter run to recover! Heck, it had even changed some hard core gear anglers into fly fisher's. Now that is what you could call a positive impact!

A little bit later that same summer/fall tied up the fly in red. Well, fish on!

The Sharp Steelie:

Hook: TMC or Targus 2457 size 8 and 6
Tail: 4 Strand Ultra Floss
Body: 4 Strand Ultra Floss
Collar: Natural Grizzly Saddle Hackle
Effective Colors: Red, Olive Green, Light Pink, White, Black,
Black with Yellow combined, Light Pink with a White tail,
Chartruese, The variations could be endless!

Tying the fly:

Step One: Attach the floss near the bend of the hook with a tag end the slightly longer than the length of the hook.

Step Two: While holding the tail in position, wrap floss back towards the hook Bend to secure the tail.

Step Three: Tightly wrap the floss towards the eye. Leave enough space for the collar and head.

Step Four: Wrap floss back just pas the middle of the body tightly.

Step Five: Wrap floss back towards the hook eye giving the body a tapered appearance.

Step Six: Attach hackle with floss and secure with one tight wrap.

Step Seven: Make 2 or 3 wraps with the hackle and secure with one tight wrap of floss.

Step Eight: Palmer hackle slightly back towards the bend of the hook. Secure with floss.

Step Nine: Make enough wraps with the floss to build the head.

Step Ten: Whip finish the head with 5 or 6 turns. Add a touch of head cement.

A couple seasons had gone by before putting the fly to test for winter runs. First time out using the light pink color ended up producing multiple fish. The red color also proved to be effective for the winter fish.

Sharp Steelie (red, light pink, and olive green)

Time to try another color, solid white. Here is what happened:

Headed out with Steve to a local river to see if we could find some late run Winter fish or possibly some very early Summer fish. The odds where stacked against us to actually find anything. I decided to try a new color of the Sharp Steelie.

We decided to go check out a canyon area on a really pristine river. We had to do a small amount of hiking. Made it to the destination without any bodily harm and commenced fly fishing.

First fish of the day ended up being a River Chub (sucker). Now that was Exciting! In just a few more cast's all hell broke loose! A very large turbo charged Steelhead slammed my fly just as it hit the water.

The fish immediately went airborne, rapidly stripped fly line and backing as it screamed towards the tail out. The fish stayed in the general area for about 5 minutes. Then things really got exciting when it decided to head for the Ocean!

Again, the fish went screaming towards the tail out, through a set of rapids with yours truly in chase while running out of backing. There was one major problem at the end of the tail out. A very large boulder that was around 20 feet high. My fly line was now on the river side of this boulder which left me with 2 choices. Hang on and pray the fish decides to turn, or go swimming. The water in this tail out was waist to chest high with some pretty strong current going right into rapids. Not to mention some very slick and medium sized rocks on the bottom.

The pretty Native above took a Pink Sharp Steelie. The fish below took the olive green.

Well, luckily I had just shorts on so all common sense went right out the window! I decided to do some water operations. At this point, my partner must think I'm totally nuts. By some kind of miracle, I actually managed to make it across the river while hanging onto a very pissed off Steelhead.

There is another version of the event where I was dragged across the river by the fish. And another saying I levitated across the water – too funny. Okay, back to the battle. Now I'm soaking wet from some very cold water and actually starting to catch up with the fish. Well, Mr. Steelhead did not like that one bit and went ripping through a second set of rapids. The chase is on again. I managed to catch up and off it went through a third set of rapids and the fish made it to a very deep pool. This time it was the end of the line with nowhere to go except into very deep, cold water. Common sense finally kicked in, fish or drown!

The only thing I could do at this point was try to ease off some pressure and hope the fish would turn. It worked, the fish turned and started to come back up river. Finally got even with the beast where I could get a good look at it. What a fish!

That did not last very long, when the mighty chromer went screaming back up through the second set of rapids. This time the fish made an error and went up a side channel. I stayed below the fish and kept on just enough pressure. While slowly working my way up to the fish it finally gave in. Wow, what a great heart wrenching battle. It was a beautiful 41 inch native buck.

After reviving and releasing the fish it stayed in the side channel for a few minutes before disappearing back into the main river. I sat and stared at the beautiful creature in complete ah.

Now, how the heck was I going to get back to the other side! Not to shabby for the first Steelhead on the White fly. Many more have now followed.

Here are some different colors, and combinations of the Sharp Steelie that have produced fish:

Black/yellow, light pink/white tail, white, yellow/black (with Elk hair wing).

Just a personal note:

The Steelhead is the ultimate endurance athlete in the fish world. Sometimes in order to understand what endurance athletes need you have to be one. Any ultra bicyclist or ultra runner understands that periodically you have replace fuel in order to finish the race. Now, while in the race it's not possible to eat a full course meal but it is possible to periodically "snack" in order to maintain energy.

Simply put, when you find Steelhead that are in the "snack" mode and use a fly pattern that imitates a food source – your odds just increased dramatically of catching Steelhead.

Pictured below: Chartruese, Patriotic (experimental), black, and salmon with red thread.

One of many large Hatchery Steelhead that was enticed by the Sharp Steelie (photo Steve Davis)

Finding Those Fish, Time To Explore

After that great first day on the North Fork of the Stillaquamish I just had to do some exploring for other opportunities. I picked up a copy of the Washington State Fishing Guide and a Washington State Atlas. Very valuable tools for any fly fisher. Whenever going to any State or Country for that matter, I make sure to pick up a fishing guide and atlas.

Ever since I was a little kid, going hiking and exploring has to be one of my favorite past times. I remember hiking in Virginia one time and finding a couple small lakes that had no road access whatsoever. They where loaded with Bass and Pan fish. I fished those little lakes for years without ever seeing another single soul. That is unless I brought someone along. If you're willing to do a little hiking and exploring it is possible to find some great Steelhead water.

Just a quick important note: make sure you have a set of regulations for any water that you plan on exploring. Read them thoroughly and make sure the water is open.

The second time out going after Steelhead, I decided to try another river. It took a little bit of time to drive and find an area to fish. I eventually stopped at what appeared to be a good area with some nice looking water. The river level was clear and low in Northwest standards so spotting fish would be somewhat easy. I must have hiked a good mile or so without spotting any signs of fish. Don't think I ever threw a single cast, so headed back to the truck and off to another area.

Well, the next area I explored was more of the same. Ran into a few anglers that had not caught any or seen any. Once again I did not even make a single cast.

This time decided to drive 10 more miles up river and see what I could find. After 10 miles it appeared the river was now further from the road. Found a small pull off and parked. Okay, this looks like some rough going with some very dense forest. I made sure the area was not private property and headed off in the direction of the river.

After what seemed like an eternity bush whacking I managed to find the river. The going was much easier once I made it to the bank. This section had a lot of boulders with pocket type water even though it was somewhat wide. Not a good place for any boats. This time, found the fish!

The first spot held 4 or 5 fish. Calmly put a cast out, guided the fly towards the fish, bingo – fish number one. Fighting a Steelhead in boulder strewn water can be quite the challenge. After a great battle managed to land the fish.

After the fight, I went back to check the same spot. There was still one fish holding. Okay, put out another cast. Worked the fly as close to the fish as possible – fish number two nailed it. This fish wasted no time and proceeded to wrap me around a boulder and came free – oh well!

I hiked down river another 50 or so yards and found some more fish.

This time it was 3 fish holding in between a couple boulders. It was quite the trick to get a fly to them, but after a couple cast's – fish on! Another wonderful battle and the fish came to hand. I went back to check the same spot. This time the fish where long gone.

After hiking down river another 50 or so yards, this time I spotted at least 10 fish sitting just below a bunch of logs. I could tell by the current that if I put the fly in just the

right spot, the current would suck it under in to the fish. Well, first cast – darn caught the log and lost a fly. Second cast, too short and missed the mark. Third cast, got it. And so did a fish. The fish was very kind and ran away from all the logs and into some open water. Another fun battle and another to hand – hey this is fun!

Well, more of the same went on for the rest of the day. I got into several fish and had a lot of fun because of a little bit of bush whacking and exploring. I made a mental note of the time of year, the area and managed to find fish at the same location every year while living in Seattle. It was work getting there, but well worth the effort.

Moving forward, on another fun outing while mountain biking along the Deschutes river I found some good stuff! As I was happily riding, kept an eye out for all kinds of wildlife including fish. There was some really good vantage points to look down into the river. Every once in a while I would notice some dark silhouettes. Made a mental note of the location, time, and date.

Of course, the very next day I had to come back with fly rod in hand. The fish where still in the same areas (might have been different fish). I ended up having another outstanding day with plenty of fish to be had. You don't have to fly fish to always find fish.

Truly have been very fortunate during my professional career to have lived in some great places in the Northwest: Seattle Washington, Astoria Oregon, Coos Bay Oregon, and Portland Oregon. While living in these area's I've been able to fish a lot of well known rivers for example; North Fork Stillaquamish, Skykomish, Skagit, Nehalem, Siletz, Elk, Roque, North Fork Umpqua, Deschutes, and the Klickitat just to name a few. Even though these rivers are well known - they don't always have a lot of fish in them; can't catch great fish if they are not there, that's why it really pays off to do some research and exploring before you go out.

Don't be afraid to call the local State Fish and Game office. They have always been more than willing to give valuable information on local rivers. Another really great source are hatcheries. They can really help turn any trip into a great one. Sometimes, when I head out to a river for the first time, will stop and talk with the people at the hatchery. Everyone that I have ever talked with has been very friendly, why not pick their minds.

A good sturdy mountain bike can really come in handy

Some rivers have old railroad tracks, dirt roads, and paved roads that run along their length. You can find a lot of great fly-fishing water by riding a bike or by hiking while enjoying some great scenery. I've located some really great area's while out on trips with the kids with no intention of fishing at all - of course it is always in the back of your mind; yes I'm guilty.

There may be some day's that running an errand, or some type of work project might just put you near a river loaded with Steelhead. It can really pay off to always be prepared.

Just this past summer had to drop a kid off and had a couple minutes to check out a river. Guess what I found – Fish On!

Another form of exploring is using various types of watercraft. Over the years the vast majority of my Steelhead fly fishing experience has been hike and fish. On some occasions, in rivers with minor rapids have used a canoe.

At river mouths there can be some great fly fishing opportunities for Steelhead. In a lot of these areas a watercraft is a must to get where the fish are. As stated in an earlier chapter, one of my most memorable day's was from a canoe. It can be quite a challenge trying to hang onto a hot Steelhead while trying to control a canoe!

In some rivers a watercraft can also get you to some water that otherwise would have no other access.

Anytime transiting a river via a canoe or any other type of watercraft, always wear a personal floatation device. Rivers have a variety of hazards that can quickly turn a wonderful day into a disaster.

I highly recommend anyone using watercraft in rivers to take some boating safety courses that may include fast water rescue. You can check with local Fire Department's,

Sheriff's, Colleges, Coast Guard Auxiliary, or other public safety organizations to find a course.

A great dirt road follows the Deschutes river – only open to hikers, bicyclists, and horseback riders.

Unlocking The Hiding Places

Just about every time I have headed out to any river, have always taken notice to the areas that the majority of fishermen fish. Most seem to prefer the deeper holes and the middle section of pools. I have to go back to my days of fly-fishing for trout in New Mexico, or for that matter any other State for trout.

A Steelhead is simply put; a Sea-run Rainbow Trout. Whenever I fly fish for Rainbows or any other species of trout for that matter in rivers, very rarely ever fish the deepest holes or the middle sections of a pool. From my experience trout like to be close to fast moving water and some type of structure and the Steelhead is no different.

There are three different area's on rivers that I have always focused on and have always produced fish:

Fish the riffles at the beginning of pools or wherever the current will allow you to get a fly down starting off with a nymphing technique. I have had Steelhead hit flies in every part of a riffle - on a dead drift, on a swing, and even when the fly is completely stopped on a straight line. Steelhead will even be in water that is only 1 or 2 feet deep if the water is choppy enough to obscure them from view. Make sure you work the entire riffle if possible.

Notice the line in the current within this riffle – Steelhead will lie on that line

The next area I look for is boulders and structure at the beginning of pools. A lot of fishermen make the mistake of only fishing behind boulders - I have actually hooked into more fish in the front of boulders than almost anywhere else. There is a small area right in front of boulders where the current tends to separate - just like a car or plane

breaking the air current. When the fish are moving up-river they seem to sit in these small pockets every time they go around a boulder or any other type of structure. I've hooked into several very large fish in these areas, including some fish over 40 inches.

   Of course you never want to overlook fishing behind and actually beside boulders. The fish could be sitting anywhere around them.
   Look for slots where the fast water meets slower water - again I'm staying at the head of a pool or more towards the tail out.
   If you don't mind losing a few flies, a log jam can be your friend. Steelhead seem to like them.
   The next area I head for is the tail out. Again, looking for boulders and structure to fish around. Also work the area where the slower water starts to speed up again at the base of pools - areas where changing current speeds usually have some fish hanging around when they are in the river.

Larger rivers can be a little bit trickier to read. Lets take the Deschutes for example. The Deschutes has a lot of very long pools and slower water in between rapids and riffles. A lot of these areas are very wide with a lot of water to cover. I've learned a couple important keys that has helped me get more hookups. First - you don't have to cast a country mile to get to the fish. Every fish that I have hooked into on this river was no more than 20 to 25 feet from the shore and some closer than that.

Second - look for areas where the current slows down and swirls in a circular pattern close to the bank. I guess the best way to describe it; it is kind of like a pool within a pool or a slow moving whirlpool. For example:

I took my brother out on the Deschutes for the first time and was trying to get him into fly fishing. Near the base of a long tail out, found an area about 15 feet from shore that was about 10 feet wide and 15 feet long that the water was slowly swirling in a circular motion - while the current around it was moving quicker. Cast my fly just above this area and the current sucked it down quickly - and then a fish quickly slammed it. A nice Steelie came flying out of the water. At that same moment my brother decided to take up fly-fishing. Now that's what I call success!

Getting away from actual areas to fish, in the past few years I have noticed something rather interesting. To the best of my knowledge and memory, have never hooked into a Steelhead before 10:00 in the morning. Yes, have gone out at the crack of dawn before and froze my butt off with everyone else. Let's just say - the past couple of years don't think I've left the house before 9:00 am to go fish any river. The majority of fish that I have landed have been smack dab in the middle of the hot afternoon. Think the key is - as the sun gets higher and hotter the fish hang out in areas where you can only get at them with a fly, and they actually get more aggressive in the afternoon! One thing I can say for sure is - it works the best when you least expect it!

Another interesting fact that I have learned in recent years is that Steelhead sometimes will go into rivers other than their home river. I have actually landed fish that were tagged from Oregon in Washington Rivers. Have also landed fish in Washington Rivers that I later found out were coming from Idaho stock. Sometimes these fish will venture into cooler rivers to take a break during their long journey.

Here is a quick list of Northwest Rivers that I have had the pleasure to fly fish for Steelhead:

In Washington;

Columbia	Skykomish
Drano Lake (Little White Salmon)	Snohomish
Green	South Fork Toutle
Klickitat	Toutle
East Fork Lewis	Washougal
North Fork Lewis	White Salmon
Pilchuck	Wind
North Fork Stillaquamish	
Sauk	
Skagit	

In Oregon;

Clackamas	Rogue
South Fork Coquille	Sandy
Deschutes	Salmon
Elk	Siletz
Klaskanine	Sixes
Lewis and Clark	Trask
Millicoma	North Fork Umpqua
Necanicum	Wilson
North Fork Nehalem	Youngs
Nestucca	

As you can tell, I still have some rivers to yet explore and try - that's always part of the fun!

Adaptation, Another Key To Success

    Learning through experience is really important when it comes to fly fishing in general and especially for Steelhead. I remember as a kid growing up, learned a lot while fishing for Largemouth Bass. During that time we used artificial worms. You had to learn how to "feel" the artificial worm. You had to learn to "feel" the subtle takes, and learn how to "work" the artificial worm in various conditions. The same goes with fly fishing. Learning to focus, feel, and work the fly is very important. Adapting to the conditions is very important. Time to go fly fishing.

    We got a typical late start on a lazy late summer day and headed for a local river. This was a somewhat large river with some pretty strong current. It was a relatively short drive and we were on the river in 35 to 40 minutes. I took a quick look around and decided on a set up.

    I went with a 7/8 weight 9 foot 6 inch fly rod with a comparable fly reel, along with a shooting head sink tip of around 15 to 18 feet in length. The main line was a weight forward 7 floating line. On the main fly line and the shooting head had attached "kevlar loop connectors" to be able to quickly shift to various types of shooting heads. The water appeared very clear, so I went with a single piece of 2x tippet material for the leader. The leader was 7 feet in length from the shooting head to the fly. I attached the leader at the shooting head with a simple improved clinch knot. Also use the same knot for the fly. (I've tried various knots but always come back to the improved clinch knot). Time to do some fishing.

We hiked down to the river and after looking around, came up with a plan of action. The first stretch of water that I decided to try had some logs at the head of the pool with some fast water coming in. The logs broke up the current as the depth of the water increased. I assessed the area and decided to go with an up river cast with some quick mending in order to get the fly where I thought the fish would be. On my first cast just about caught one of the logs but quickly figured out where to place the next one (There where some amused onlookers on the other side of the river). The next cast I managed to put the fly and fly line in a position that would aid in getting the fly down beneath the logs. I had to do some quick mending (both up and down river) to help reduce the drag from the current. I was basically using a "nymphing" technique in this section of river.

Well, it worked. Managed to hook up with a beautiful Steelhead from below the logs to the amusement of some anglers on the other bank. The fish took me quite some distance down river before bringing it to hand. I carefully revived and released the fish and headed back to the same area.

After a few more cast's around the logs with no more takes, I decided to move down river a short distance.

 From within the same stretch of water and just slightly down stream from the logs I could barely make out what appeared to be a shelf. Just down river of the shelf appeared to be some boulders off the bottom. The water was a little bit slower but was still somewhat deep – guessing around 15 feet of so. Okay, now I had to switch tactics. The goal was to try and drift the fly along the shelf and swing it in front of the boulders. This time would have to cast slightly up river and with a little less mending to achieve the goal.

 After a few cast's managed to put the fly where I wanted it. Just as the fly started to swing a fish nailed it. Off to the races we went. This one went straight for the tail out and quickly made a U turn back up river. The fish ended up staying in the upper third of the pool for most of the battle. Eventually another nice fish came to hand. Sometimes where there is one there may be another.

 I headed back to the same area, using the same technique – another fish! It's turning out to be a good day with some good action. Well, I tried the same area again for a few minutes with no more success. Time to move.

 Avoiding the middle section of the pool, next stop was the tail out. As I was working my way down, scouted the water to look for signs of fish. I did not spot any fish in the tail out but went ahead with a few casts. Sometimes you just can't spot them. This water was guessing around 3 to 4 feet deep with the current getting stronger. Now my cast was going straight across the river with minimal mending. The goal was to swing the fly across the tail out with the speed of the fly slightly slower and at times slightly faster than the current. I was able to achieve this with different sizes of the "bow" in the line as the fly swung across the current. Another trick is to follow the fly line with the rod tip at different levels.

 After no takes in the tail out, it was time to move again. Next stop, my personal favorite type of water!

    The next area was a wonderful, wide, fast moving riffle water with some various depths. Guessing most was around 2 ½ to 4 feet deep. There was also some slots and various sized rocks. As Steelhead move up this type of water they will at times hold along some of the larger rocks or duck into a slot. This is also the type of water where I like to work the entire section. The current in this particular section was still strong enough to get away with a sinking shooting head.

    Time to shift tactics again. I cast straight across the river, one quick mend to get the fly down near the bottom quick. Allow the line to tighten. As the line is starting to come across the river, start to raise the rod tip until the fly is eventually bouncing on the surface. Allow the fly to make it all the way to the same bank. Hang on and be prepared for some vicious takes!

    Basically, what I'm trying to do is: Start the fly deep and allow it to rise as it crosses the current and also allow it to skate. Can be very exciting! Back to fishing.

    It didn't take long to have a fish smash my fly in the riffle water. The first one smacked the fly on the surface. Actually saw the tail of the fish before it hit, coming straight at the fly like a torpedo. What a total rush! Well, this time must not have got a very good hook set. It was only on for about 15 seconds or so. Bummer, I could tell it was a large one – oh well.

    The next fish that hit the fly came straight out of the water like it was on a pogo stick! This time the fly was almost at the surface when the fish smacked it. The fly had just passed over and slightly behind a good size rock that was almost breaking the surface. I love it when those fish come from underneath a fly and slam them. Fun time, big time! This time I got a good hook set and brought the beauty to hand.

Just a little hint: When skating a fly across or near the surface, when the fish hits it – don't yank! Allow the force of the hit to hook the fish or you could pull the fly free.

Well, more of the same continued throughout the day with plenty of fish to be had. I managed to effectively stick with the same set up all day while changing tactics. Adapting to the conditions, and being willing to change, can make a day very successful.

The same tactics can also be very effective when using a floating line, especially in smaller rivers with weak currents. The only thing that I change is the length of the leader. I go with 3 feet of 0x, 3 feet of 1x, and 4 feet or greater of 2x. Either a blood knot to attach the sections together, or loops created with a double surgeons knot do the trick.

Results from adapting to the conditions, another nice fish.

Get Ready To Rumble

Now it's show time. In my opinion there is nothing that compares to hooking into a fresh Steelhead on a fly rod - there is a reason it is considered the Premier Fresh Water Game Fish in North America if not the World. I've had this uncanny ability to be very lucky to have landed an incredible amount of fish and every single one has been a major challenge and fun! Here are some keys that have helped me to land this incredible fighter.

In my years of fly fishing one thing I have noticed is that a lot of anglers tend to get a little over excited and put to much pressure on themselves to land the fish.

This might sound a little odd, but every time I head out to a river I don't expect to land fish. My whole goal is to hook into some fish and have a great and enjoyable battle. Because I don't have any expectations, I don't put myself under pressure to actually land any fish. And you know what - it works!

I have to pick on one of my friends for a moment just to emphasize what I'm trying to get across. We were on a great river and my partner hooked into his first fish of the day and I think his first fish on a fly rod. Well I think adrenaline and excitement took over because in a matter of seconds my partner managed to wrap himself in his fly line and almost went swimming while the fish did what a Steelhead does best - went bananas. Well you can guess it, the fish wasn't on very long, and I swear on one jump it actually stuck its tongue out at my partner. It was truly a very comical start to the day and we had a great chuckle over it. Lessons learned: when a fish hits your fly - stay calm!

When a fish first hits my fly I try to very lightly lift my rod tip without applying a lot of pressure - the majority of the time these fish have hit my flies so hard I basically just hang on! The first few seconds are critical in my opinion and I do my best not to apply too much pressure on the fish. Let them run and be ready to chase them - that's the fun part. It is also very important to get all the fly line on the reel as soon as you can and try to keep the slack out. Remember; stay calm. Sometimes I will even yawn to keep myself calm.

When these fish are running upriver it can actually be a benefit - don't put to much pressure on them. You can actually tire them out quicker on long upriver runs and you will have a better chance of actually landing it. By just keeping slight pressure on, the fish is fighting the current and the fly rod - if you turn them to quick and they start screaming down river to soon they may not stop until they reach the sea! I try to keep my rod at about a 10 o'clock position while fighting the fish unless it runs for some type of structure where it could break off.

When a fish starts heading down river I try my best not to put too much pressure on, and only enough to tell you actually have one on the line. Sometimes this can actually get the fish to turn around and has worked for me about 80 percent of the time. If this means that I have to quickly chase the fish by running with them instead of applying too much pressure with the fly rod than that's what I will do. Hey, might as well get in a good workout!

    I think the major key to fighting these fish on a fly rod is finesse and not trying to out power them. Of course there is the other 20 percent when you just have to chase the fish and hope you don't run out of room. I've actually climbed along some small cliffs and gone over some very large boulders chasing fish. Not to mention having to actually swim a time or two!

    If any fish species on the planet was the genius it has to be the Steelhead. Every time you think you have these fish warn out - watch out. A major mistake is trying to land them to soon. Every time you get a Steelhead near the beach be prepared for another explosive run. Don't get caught with your fly rod to high or to low, and don't have your drag locked down to the point it would cause your tippet to easily break. Bottom line - be prepared to battle the fish just as if it just hit your fly, and again - stay calm, enjoy the battle.

    I've had some fish right at the shore after a lengthy battle, getting ready to tail them and they exploded! Got me soaking wet, and had to fight them for several more minutes. I'm always ready for the fish to take off again every time it is near the shore - that's part of the fun and challenge!

    Something to keep in mind; Steelhead are cold water fish and prefer water temperatures below 60 degrees. When the water temperature starts to hover around 65 degrees it can quickly become life threatening for the fish. A lengthy battle could prove to be fatal for any fish that are going to be released.

    After a wonderful battle care should be taken for any fish that are going to be released. The vast majority of river systems containing Steelhead, the wild fish must be released, check the appropriate regulations. Steelhead as with any other Trout or Salmon are very valuable resources. We need to take care of them.

 When releasing the fish, gently cradle the fish with one hand just slightly behind the gills near the pectoral fins. With the second hand hold the fish just in front of the tail fin. Keep the head of the fish facing into the current. This will increase the amount of oxygenated water over the fish's gills. Make sure to get the fish in an upright normal swimming position quickly. Once the fish has regained it's strength, gently release it facing into the current.

Holding the fly rod at a good angle while palming the fly reel rim.

A Wonderful Fall Day – Dreams Can Come True

It started off as a typical day while getting the opportunity to head for my favorite river. I had to help prepare the kids for school and drop my son off on the way out. With the typical late start and a good drive of over an hour to get to the river, I hit the road. Nice thing was I had the afternoon and evening completely open.

I really lucked out because the weather was absolutely perfect. There was no wind, the temperature was in the low 50's and I knew it would warm up upon reaching the river. Heck, just happy to drive through the Columbia River Gorge and enjoy the scenery, stunning!

After making it to my favorite destination I took a look around the river mouth. Hmmm, only a few boats around. Well it was a weekday, so I decided to drive up river to do a little exploring.

At the first stop it was just a very short hike to the river. The air temperature was now around 58-60 degrees and it was already 10:45am. I took a deep breath and soaked up the surroundings while setting up the fly gear. I've not even thrown a cast yet and it's already perfect! Even the color of the water was great, a beautiful turquoise blue.

After scouting the run from a good vantage point, I started to hike up towards the first water to try out. While hiking, I became so focused on the water that I ended up having a bonding relationship with a rock. Well, there went the perfect morning while proceeding to do a complete end over. A few cuts and bruises no big deal – the fly rod was okay! It truly is important to learn how to walk prior to fly casting.

Okay, the first area to hit was at the head of the pool with some boulders scattered here and there. I carefully waded out through the ice cold water (it felt good on the minor cuts) and commenced casting to some fishy looking water. Was basically working the area all around the boulders. After just a few cast's, hooked into the first fish of the day.

The fish made a couple great jumps and ran straight for the tail out. It had a golden/silver coloration with just a slight touch of pink hue. I wasn't sure if it was a Steelhead or perhaps a Coho Salmon. After reaching the tail out (without stumbling), the fish made a couple more jumps. This time I was sure it was a Coho. It gave me a good battle so I had nothing to complain about – even if it wasn't a Steelhead. Hey, a fish is a fish!

After the battle, I headed back up to the same area. It did not take very long to hook into another fish, and it was another Coho. This fish was much darker than the first and did not put up a very good fight. Then I thought to myself, if the Salmon are in this area, maybe there is some Steelhead sitting below them. Steelhead will sit below Salmon and eat up some lose eggs – hmmm.

I moved down the river about 20 feet from where the Coho's had taken the fly. At the time I had on a red fly and even though it did not match the egg color, went ahead and stuck with it. I waded back out just a small distance and put a cast out to some good fish holding water. This time it only took one cast when a fish erupted with the fly. There was no doubt – it was a Steelhead. The fish took me on a great up river run, right through the area that held the salmon, into some riffle water while dancing in between some boulders. What a fun fish! It was quite the challenge trying to keep the fly line from getting wrapped around the boulders. The fish gave it a valiant effort with the "boulder dance". I was eventually able to work the fish towards some calmer water and tailed a wonderful scrappy small Steelhead.

Where there is one, there may be another I thought to myself. I went straight back to the same exact spot.

After a few more minutes of casting I noticed a dark object coming through the air out of the corner of my eye. I stopped paying attention to fly fishing as an incredible Golden Eagle came flying across my path. The bird was only about 15 feet or so above the water and only about 25 feet from where I was standing. Wow, what an amazing creature. I was totally engrossed in watching the eagle, when it happened again.

The fish about ripped the fly rod out of my hands, I lost my balance and took a bath in the very cold water. Of course my body did not matter, the only thing that really counted was to keep pressure on the fly rod. Somehow, managed to keep the fish on as I stumbled back to a standing position. The eagle must have been amused with all the commotion because it stayed around. So here I am soaking wet, still watching the eagle while hanging onto a Steelhead. Maybe the eagle was looking for a free meal. Actually the bird was most likely enjoying a stupid human trick. After another fun battle, tailed another Steelhead.

Well, maybe third time in the same spot is a charm. I thoroughly worked the same area for about 10 more minutes with no more takers. Wading down about 10 feet as the water was starting to slow a little bit, I looked for some seams and current breaks and commenced casting again. Within just a few cast's, another fish was off to the races (think the eagle got bored after 5 minutes with no action and left).

Now this Steelhead wasted no time. It bolted straight for the boulders up river making a bunch of leaps as it traveled. Then it quickly made a figure eight around some boulders and was gone! That was a smart fish and quickly reminded me of the word "luck". I had absolutely no chance this time.

No problem, back to the drawing board to try and find another. Again, where there is one there may be more. Within just a few more cast's, another fish erupted. After another wonderful battle, managed to tail another fish without incident.

I worked the same stretch of water for a little while longer with no more takes. After all the action within this stretch of water it confirmed something to me. If there is Salmon present, Steelhead may be just below them. Time to move.

I hiked back to the vehicle to head upriver a few more miles and scout some new areas. As I was driving along noticed a familiar looking vehicle parked by the river and decided to pull in and check things out.

The truck belonged to a gent who runs a local fly shop close to home. He was taking a lunch break and I thought that was a good idea. We chatted for a little bit and I found out he was not having very good luck. He had just worked the stretch of water where we were parked with nothing. At the time I didn't have the heart to tell him what happened just a short distance down river. After finishing a late lunch, he left and drove up river and I decided to go ahead and give the same section of river a try.

This time I decided to go with a light pink Sharp Steelie fly. After getting set up, I hiked up the river just a short distance. I found a good looking area with some boulders along with various currents. I started casting and working the water.

As I was working the fly, kept getting bumps but for some reason was not hooking up. Couldn't figure out what the heck was going on when finally I hooked a fish. It fought hard for all of 10 seconds and all of a sudden it felt small. After a very short battle, I ended up catching a White Fish.

I decided to try the same area again. Once again hooked and landed another White Fish. Then I thought to myself – maybe just maybe some Steelhead or Salmon might be just above the White Fish.

Well, that was good thinking. I waded up river about 15 to 20 feet above the area that was holding White Fish. First cast in the new spot, Steelhead on! Off to the races as the fish ripped me into my backing as it blistered down stream. There was a nice long slow moving pool just below the boulders where the fish settled in. It was a nice change of pace because this section was basically easy to work a fish. After tailing the fish I quickly figured there was some fish in this stretch after all. Where there is one, there might just be more.

I hiked back up river to the same section and started where the last Steelhead was hooked. After about 15 minutes or so another fish was on. This fish did almost the same exact motions as the first one and basically gave me a very manageable battle. I tailed the second fish and decided to try the same area again.

This time I worked the section for a good 30 to 45 minutes with no more takes. Had always thought if I ran into White Fish there might be Steelhead or Salmon just above them. Just like the Steelhead hanging below Salmon when they are in the river together. Think I got some confirmation.

Next stop – time to head for the tail out. I hiked back down river and by passed the section where the previous couple fish where tailed. While I was hiking, tried to keep a sharp look out for any fish. The water was just to deep and not quite clear enough to make out any fish.

I made it to the tail out and carefully waded out a short distance to be able to cast. As I was wading kept a close look out for the possibility of any spawning reds. Not a good idea to disturb any fish that may be in the act of spawning. The area was clear of spawning fish so was hoping to find a fish moving up.

Well, it took a little bit of time to work a good size tail out. Just as I was thinking about calling it quits, a Steelhead smacked my fly as I was retrieving it. The fish headed straight for the middle section of the pool and settled in just as the first two. Again, another

very manageable battle with some nice jumps and always excitement. It was now late afternoon, I had just tailed another fish and was very satisfied. Time to head home.

As I was happily driving home, already tired and very satisfied noticed another section of river that looked interesting. The river beckoned me to visit once more. It was like some type of trance and would not let go even at the stage of exhaustion. I gave in.

After parking, got my stuff together once more and now stumbled towards the river. It was like some kind of magnetic traction beam that pulled me along. Still have a long drive, what the heck am I doing.

There was a wonderful section of water where a tail out came into a really nice riffle. I decided to stick with the pink fly and started out at the base of the tail out. First cast, a large Chinook took off with my fly. This thing was a tank with fins and I knew it was going to be a long one.

It was a slow, long, hard fought tug of war when the fish finally started to give in. It had taken a good 200 to 300 yards down river to an area that had some back water. As I finally got the beast near the shore another angler helped to corral it. The fish was in good enough shape to keep but decided to turn it loose to the shock of some onlookers.

Alright, now I'm really tired, my arm is hurting and the last thing I wanted to do was hook another Chinook. Got myself together and started to head for the truck. Then it happened again. The river would just not release me. The pull was overwhelming and I just couldn't fight it. Had to do another cast.

I dragged myself back upriver to the riffle water all the while thinking I must be nuts! Somehow found the energy to change out the tippet and tied on the pink fly. I made a cast across the riffle water and allowed the fly to bounce on the surface. Followed the fly line with my rod tip raised until the line stopped. Just as I made one single strip, with the fly bouncing around on the surface it happened!

The largest eruption of water from a fish that I have ever witnessed! My first thought was, what the heck is a Tarpon doing in the Northwest. When the fish hit I was holding the fly line in my left hand. In a matter of seconds I saw backing while my left hand is now bleeding from the line burn. I woke up from a state of shock and started to run.

The fish had covered the same 200 to 300 yards as the Chinook in a matter of minutes with jumps like a missile coming out of a submarine. Thank goodness I was into cycling and in descent shape. There would have been no way I could have run with that fish otherwise. As I caught up, it turned and covered the same distance as it ran back to the riffles. I was at the complete mercy of the fish and could only hang on and run. It ran through the riffles, into the next tail out and into the next pool as I hung on. I managed to get even with it, while it was on the other side of the pool – a good 150 feet across.

Then it took off again on another incredible down river run. I literally had to sprint to keep up – was in complete ah at the power of this fish. Goes without saying, I'm no longer in an exhaustive state with the adrenaline in high gear. What soar arm, its focus time.

The fish ran back down river through the riffles and this time eased up after a couple hundred yards. Still with the same pace but less jumps. Again as I got even with it, it bolted back up river, went back through the riffles again and stopped in the large pool. As it took off, by the time I was able to react the backing was zinging through the snake guides. As I'm thinking, oh I hope my tippet holds up. It was a 2x. As the sun starts to set, once again I catch up with the fish in the upper pool.

   This time the fish stays in the pool for a few minutes and I thought it might be starting to tire. As soon as I thought that, here we go again. Another amazing down river run with the fish doing the missile thing again. This is totally surreal. Pretty soon darkness is going to set in and I will no longer be able to see where to run!

   The fish stops after another couple hundred yard run and again allows me to catch up. Now I'm really starting to think the tippet is going to give way. Again, another U turn and off to the races. Back through the riffles and back into the upper pool. This time the fish did not break the surface. Maybe, just maybe might finally have a chance to bring it in. Wrong answer! As I got even with the fish – it did it again!

   Another what started off as a blistering run, the fish seemed to go on cruise control after about 125 yards. I was able to catch up while it was still heading down river this time. The fish took me another 150 yards down river as it seemed to be doing a search pattern. The zigzag pattern went on for what felt like an eternity. Finally the fish just seemed to go into slow motion as swam straight towards me. As it approached, I finally got the first good look at it. I was dumbfounded by the shear enormity of it. Then the amazing Steelhead swam right around a corner into the back water where the most exhilarating fly fishing battle of my life came to an end. Just as the colors of the day faded into obscurity.

   I then drove home in a euphoric trance. The day was done. When the river speaks – listen.

A fish of dreams

Show me the splash!

It's The Technique, Not The Equipment

When it comes to successfully fly fishing for Steelhead it starts with the Fly Fisher. Next, I believe the most important piece of equipment is the fly itself. From there it moves on to the fly rod, fly reel, fly line, and various other equipment. Fly fishing can actually be very affordable to anyone, irregardless of income. It does not matter to the fish what type of fly rod, fly reel, fly line etc. But the fly pattern sure does.

Over the years, I have personally been using some very modest equipment that has performed very well. Of course, it would be nice to own some top of the line stuff, but sometimes that's just not possible.

Along that same line, personally tend to be a little bit rough on equipment because of exploring. I like to do a little bit of rock and tree climbing to find good water. Having equipment that I'm not worried about banging up is a plus.

With fly rods my main criteria is: sensitivity, ability to cast, able to take abuse, strong enough to handle large fish, and cost. Then it's time to do some comparing. For Steelhead, a good 7 to 9 weight single hand fly rod from 9 to 10 feet is a good start. I prefer a 7 weight 9'6" graphite fly rod. When large Salmon are present I prefer a 9 weight 9'6" graphite fly rod with a thin tip. My 7 weight is an IM6 graphite and 9 weight is a C44X graphite. They are both relatively inexpensive, have a fighting butt, and work great.

It really can be a lot of fun to test out a wide variety of fly rods. While shopping around the last thing I look at is the price. If the fly rod is not affordable, move on until finding one with the right feel at the right price. Another option is to build your own starting from rod blanks. Now there is nothing wrong with dreaming and drooling over a certain fly rod. Personally, wish I had a Bamboo fly rod that could hold up to fight a mighty Steelhead with. Sometimes it's just not possible and that's okay!

The main job of a fly reel is to simply hold the fly line. For Steelhead, it does need to be able to hold a good 150 to 200 yards of backing. Having a fly reel with an exposed spool rim is also very important in my opinion. A strong drag system is a nice plus. Last but not least, balance with the fly rod is a good thing (7/8 fly reel for a 7/8 fly rod etc). By doing some good comparing and shopping, it is possible to find a relatively inexpensive fly reel to fit the bill. Of course it would be nice to have a dream reel to fit the dream fly rod. But hey, it does not have to be the best to do the job.

Now with fly lines, I think a high quality line is very important. If I had to spend less on a fly rod and reel to get a higher quality line, than that is the route I would go. Good durable fly lines with high abrasion resistance are crucial. I use a good quality WF floating fly line along with good quality sinking shooting head lines. Have set up a system were I can quickly interchange different lengths of shooting head sink tips. There are some good quality pre-made systems that are now on the market. With my own system, I use kevlar loop connectors with some strong rubber adhesive to secure them. It has held up to some very large fish and is less expensive then the pre-made systems. I also use different sink rate shooting head tips for various conditions.

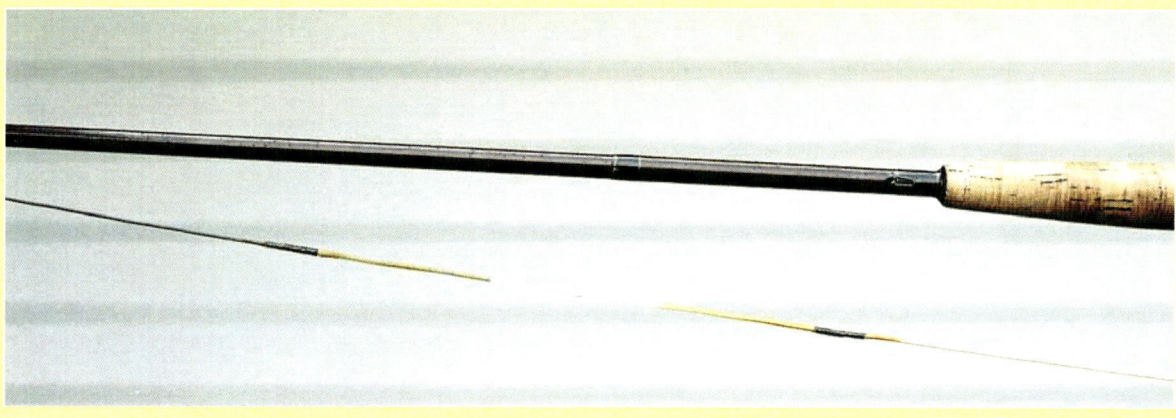

My very first fly fishing outfit for Steelhead included a good graphite fly rod, a fly reel that met all the necessary requirements, a good fly line and backing for under a hundred bucks. Now that was back in 1986 and the same equipment still works today. It's still possible to find equipment these day's for relatively low cost that will do the job. That leads to fly shops.

A good fly shop should be able to help set someone up whether they only have say 150 bucks or 500 bucks to spend. If you don't have enough money to afford a fly rod, fly reel, fly line, set up – a good shop will set you up with other avenues in order to be able to enjoy the art of fly fishing. Just makes good sense for some reason. With that said, please support your local shop when able to – they are very valuable resources.

There is many other options to obtaining equipment: Catalogue stores, on-line internet shopping, sporting good stores, used equipment through clubs etc. If someone only has a very minimal amount of funds – there is a way to get into fly fishing.

When it comes to flies, fly tying is the way to go (of course that's coming from a fly tier). It can be a little spendy to get started but will pay off in the long run. If you have a little bit of patience, just a smidgen of creativeness, and a tiny bit of time – go for it! Even tying a pattern that someone else came up with, it's still your work. There is nothing like catching fish on flies that you tied. It's not for everyone, but if there is just a tiny bit of interest, give it a try. I always start with the fly and work back words!

Now, once that first Steelhead comes on the fly rod – your toast and there is no turning back. Just going to have to get a good fly vest and all kinds of wonderful gadgets and gizmos to go along. A good luck hat is a must.

Here are some must have goodies: Polarized glasses, multi tools, scissors, finger nail clippers, fly boxes, locking forceps, hook file, water thermometer, small needle nose pliers, rain jacket, assortment of tippet material, just to name a few.

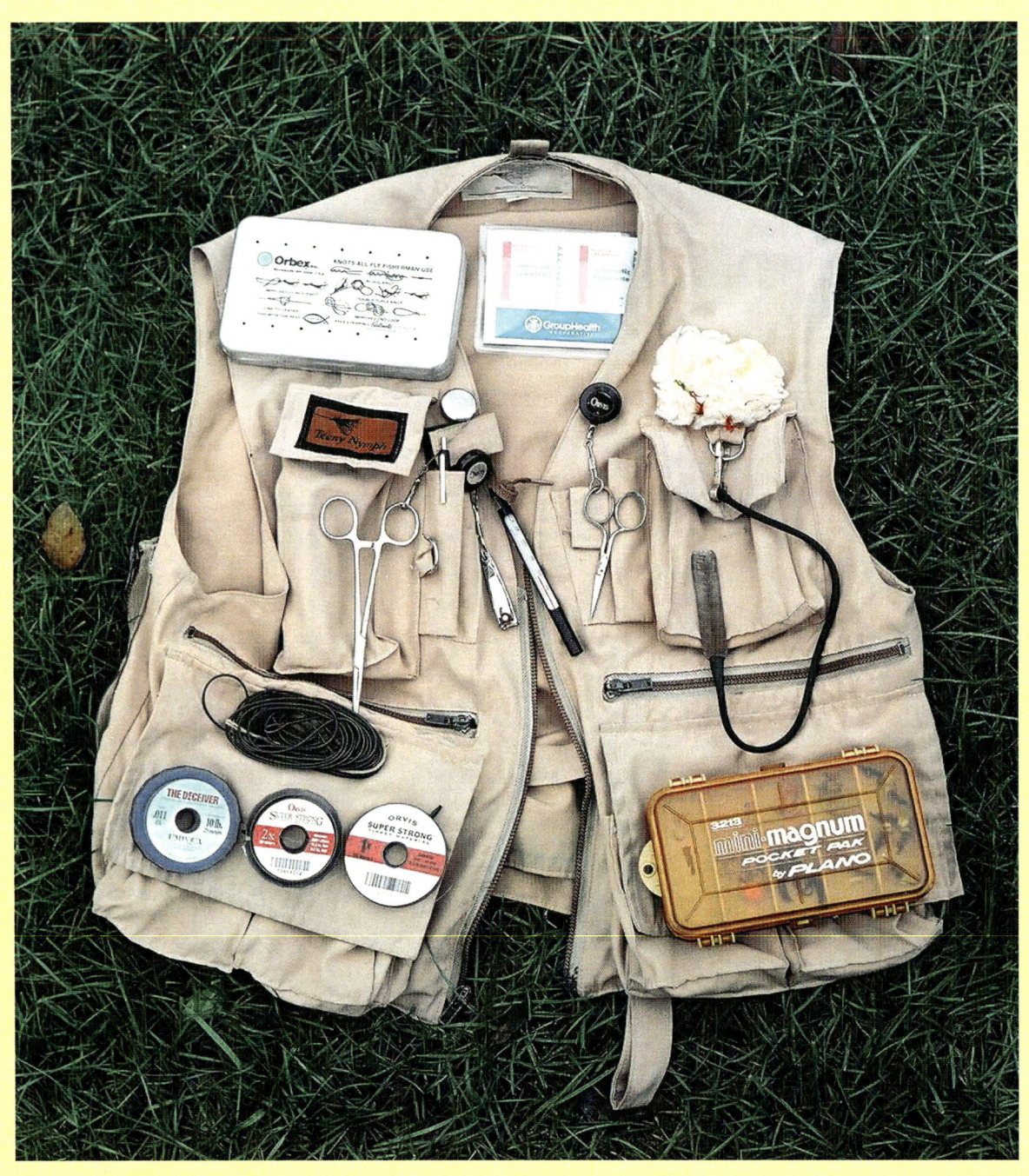

Something else that I always carry along in the vehicle is a well stocked first aid kit. You just never know when it might be needed.

If going after winter run fish, waders are a must. These days there is a variety of wader types to fit the bill. Neoprene waders can be found for a very reasonable price. The newer breathable waders are a little bit more spendy but are rather nice. Personally, I prefer to wade in shorts, and wading boots until the air temp just gets to cold. Easier to chase a fish in shorts!

It truly is possible to get set up to fly fish for Steelhead at a minimal cost. Of course upgrading can be fun when the opportunity is there.

The fly fisher catches the fish. The equipment is merely the tool to make it happen.

What Good Is Treasure If You Can't Share It

For many years while serving with the United States Coast Guard, fly fishing had become my escape from the pressures of life. Fly fishing had become an avenue of personal replenishment. It was a time to become one with my Creator and the beautiful nature around us.

As time went on, developed my own unique style, methods, and techniques. Literally, the fly rod had become an extension of my arm and a part of my body. I had learned how to feel and how to become completely in tune with the surroundings. It was like painting a picture while in the picture itself.

While stationed in Astoria Oregon with the Coast Guard, I had a wonderful fishing partner – Al Rice.

Al was the Pastor at Seaside Christian Church. Not only did we fish together, we also lead music at the Church. Al used to joke with me that I could single handedly feed the congregation if we kept all the fish that I caught. He also said jokingly "I was blessed with a special touch". That was quite a while ago and Al is no longer with us on this earth. I know he is smiling down from some happy fishing waters. It has been many years since living in the Astoria area, yet the magic has continued.

Since moving to the Portland Oregon area for the second time it brought some new awakenings and challenges in fly fishing. I had basically lived what most only dream about when it comes to fly fishing for Steelhead. Funny thing, had no clue until some people pointed it out. Was just going out catching fish, and having fun. Basically just kept to myself for a very long time. It was after inviting some others to try my stuff out that I finally figured was really on to something.

I had invited Steve to do some fishing with me and he had never used a fly rod for Steelhead before. Well, was doing my normal thing and getting into a bunch of fish. Ended up with the opportunity to show him what I was doing and the next thing you know – With just a little bit of coaching, Steve got his first fly rod Steelhead using my fly rod and flies.

Steve with a nice fish
(Photo by Mike Ellsworth)

Same summer and next time out I bring my son along for his first Steelhead fly fishing trip. Tyler was 8 years old at the time. We managed to get him a fish his first time out. Dang – he is really ahead of the game!

Tyler and Dad with a nice one
(Photo by Ben Knapp)

A few weeks later, still the same summer. Denny decided to try out the fly fishing thing with me. Steve had also come along and the three of us headed out. We had decided to bring some hatchery fish home this particular day for the families if there was any around.

After tailing several fish I decided to take a break and set Denny up. After some quick instruction, Denny nailed his first fly rod Steelhead his first time out. It ended up being another really fun day. Luckily, we all were able to justify the fly fishing trip with some fresh fish for the families – whew! This is awesome, my flies and techniques are working for others – what a great season.

Denny's first fly fishing trip with Clay
(Photo by Steve Davis)

A couple more years had passed when Toby came by to install some cable one day. He had noticed a couple pictures with fish and asked about them. After a long conversation he decided to go get set up with a fly fishing outfit the very next day. We went out the following week and it happened again. After observing my fly fishing style, with a little bit of coaching, and a very effective fly – Toby tailed his first Steelhead. This was his first time ever trying a fly rod for Steelhead. Toby also tailed his first 40" Steelhead his first season fly fishing for Steelhead. The beast took a pink Sharp Steelie fly.

On another fun trip ended up with another opportunity to share fly fishing with a young gentleman. I had already landed several fish when Austin asked me about fly fishing. With some quick on stream instruction, using my equipment, Austin got his first Steelhead with a fly rod. Kids are really quick learners!

I have a lot of respect for anyone who helps kids out. Sean is one of many people who coaches a variety of kids sports. We met on a river after both having a pretty long drive. Guess what happened. It was an honor to witness him tail his first Steelhead with a fly rod.

Sean's first fly rod Steelie

Even more important than catching Steelhead myself, I have learned that it is pure joy to help others. The facial expressions that I have witnessed as someone hooks their first Steelhead while fly fishing – priceless! That's what this book is all about.

Austin's first fly rod Steelhead

Now this is what I would call a very happy camper. This particular fly fishing trip with Toby produced some huge hatchery Steelhead that where taken on the Sharp Steelie. After another incredible day of fly fishing, we were then treated with a beautiful sun set while driving through stunning country. It truly was another season of magical fly fishing for the majestic Steelhead.

Toby holding a pair of very large hatchery Steelhead